MW00445989

eat.shop washington dc

second edition : researched, photographed and written by
anna h. blessing

cabazon books : 2008

table of contents

eat

shop

anna's notes on dc

i had my first taste of washington, d.c., when i was seven years old, while visiting the nation's capitol with my family. we saw the jefferson memorial, waited in line to ogle the declaration of independence and took pictures of the washington monument. we strolled the national mall, admired the capitol building, toured the white house and even caught a glimpse of president reagan. but the single most striking memory i have from that inaugural trip was a taste: freeze-dried neapolitan ice cream from the national air and space museum. freeze-dried ice cream may not seem worthy to compete with the great monuments of america, or crossing paths with the leader of the free world, but my tongue was impressed.

at the time i had no way of knowing that this city would become best known to me through its flavors. though most people plan their dc trip to fit in the many sights, my days here are spent trying to fit in more than three meals a day, while sniffing out the most interesting shopping between. show me a map, and i will lead you not to the many memorials, monuments and museums; but to menudos, mussels and mojitos; mercury glass, marshmallow sofas and marimekko towels.

the way i best experience—and remember—a place is through experiencing the local eating and shopping establishments. two years ago, i sought out some of this city's most unusual and memorable spots for the first edition of *eat.shop washington dc*. for this second edition, i couldn't wait to return to beloved businesses and of course, discover new ones. whether you're a native of dc or a visitor, i hope you will enjoy exploring these amazing spots, as well as finding your own special places along the way.

when i'm not devouring and coveting, here are a few of my favorite things to do in dc:

1 > *visit the corcoran gallery of art*: one of the oldest museums in the country that houses an amazing collection of american, european and contemporary art, and has an excellent café to boot.

2 > *go undercover at the international spy museum*: espionage, who-dunnits and spy secrets throughout history—who doesn't love a spy story?

3 > *ride the metro*: this is one of the best ways to get around town, with the bonus of admiring the stately, symmetric stations designed by architect harry weese.

4 > *walk the mall*: you can see everything from here, from the u.s. capitol to the washington monument.

5 > *tour the national air and space museum*: don't miss the wright 1903 flyer, the spirit of st. louis, or of course, the freeze-dried neapolitan ice cream.

a. litteri, inc.

italian grocer and deli

517-519 morse street northeast. between fifth and sixth
red: new york ave / florida ave / gallaudet u
202.544.0183 www.litteris.com
tue - wed 8a - 4p thu - fri 8a - 5p sat 8a - 3p

opened in 1926. owner: michael defrancisci
$: mc. visa
grocery. deli. first come, first served

near northeast > e01

The best way to get the best goods is to go straight to the source. And the source in DC for drool-worthy Italian foods is this decades-old Italian grocery. It's like entering an age of old at *A. Litteri*, tucked away amid the factories and the food warehouses. Even though it looks tiny from the outside, inside is stacked floor-to-ceiling with pastas, olives, oils and wines. But the tastiest treat of all is to be found in the back deli where prosciutto, mortadella, salami and capicola are piled high to create foot-long subs—it's an old-world taste of heaven. *Che incredibile—qui si mangia bene*!

imbibe I devour:
anna pasta
modena balsamic vinegar
cento canned tomatoes
illy coffee
parma prosciutto
soppresata
a hundred extra virgin olive oils!

amsterdam falafel shop

munchies nirvana

2425 18th street northwest. between belmont and columbia
red: woodley park-zoo / adams morgan
202.234.1969 www.falafelshop.com
sun - mon 11a - midnight tue - wed 11a - 2:30a thu 11a - 3a fri - sat 11a - 4a

opened in 2004. owners: scott and arianne bennett
$: cash
lunch. dinner. late night. first come, first served

adams morgan > **e02**

Good things come in threes. I wholeheartedly believe this and often do things in threes, including daily errands. When I saw that the menu at *Amsterdam Falafel* consisted of three things: falafel, frites and virgin brownies, I hoped it would be the ideal trifecta. Now I find myself craving this falafel, not to mention the twice-fried fries dipped in housemade mayonnaise—an indulgence that even I, a non-mayo eater, couldn't get enough of. Once you've had the first two items, you must end with the third. Virgin, indeed, but you might find yourself equally high at the end of this meal.

imbibe / devour:
falafel
garnishes:
  pickled cucumbers
  pickled beets
  turkish salad
  fried eggplant
frites with mayonnaise
virgin brownies

baked and wired

coffee, tea and unbelievable baked stuff

1052 thomas jefferson street northwest. between m and k
orange / blue: foggy bottom / gwu
202.333.2500 www.bakedandwired.com
mon - fri 7a - 7p sat 10a - 7p sun 11a - 6p

opened in 2001. owner: teresa velazquez
$: all major credit cards accepted
coffee. treats. first come, first served

georgetown > **e03**

If I were to rename *Baked & Wired*, I would give it the moniker of *Yummiest Most Delicious Best Baked Goods on the Planet*. When customers came in they would think to themselves, "Oh well, we'll just see about that now, won't we?" Then they would order a cupcake and a bee sting and a piece of cardamom coffee cake for good measure and then they would devour them all and they would understand and agree that the name was correct—as this is the most absurdly delicious place around to eat sweet treats.

imbibe / devour:
baked & wired blend coffee
iron goddess of mercy tea
bee stings
pumpkin ginger bread
cardamom coffee cake
ginger sugar cookie
strawberry rhubarb pie
fresh peach cream pie

bar pilar

neighborhood saloon

1833 14th street northwest. between s and t

green: u street / african-american civil war memorial / cardozo

202.265.1751 www.barpilar.com

mon 5 - 10p tue - sat 5 - 11p brunch sun 11a - 4p bar open nightly until 2a

opened in 2005. owner: mike benson chef: justin bittner

$$: all major credit cards accepted

brunch. lunch. dinner. first come, first served

I like to branch out and explore new places to eat and drink outside of my neighborhood, but when it comes down to it, my favorite, regular places are those in my own hood—the gems that visitors and travelers are likely to miss. When I travel to another city, I like to try to root out these spots. DC is a city full of neighborhood restaurants, but one of my favorites is *Bar Pilar*. It feels like one extended group of friends hanging out here, sharing small plates and enjoying an after-work drink. I call this good ol' fashioned neighborhood love.

imbibe / devour:
allagash white beer
magic hat #9 beer
blanched radishes with amish country butter
exotic mushrooms & braised leeks
fried quail with truffled polenta fries
rabbit casoulet, confit, seared loin & pork sausage
calamari with tomato basil sauce
cheese & charcuterie plate

ben's chili bowl

dc chili institution

1213 u street northwest. between 13th and 12th
green: u st / african-american civil war memorial / cardozo
202.667.0909 www.benschilibowl.com
breakfast mon - fri 6 - 11a sat 7 - 11a
lunch / dinner mon - thu 11 - 2a fri - sat 11 - 4a sun 11a - 8p

opened in 1958. owners: kamal and nizam ali
$: all major credit cards accepted
breakfast. lunch. dinner. first come, first served

u street > e05

After the first eat.shop dc book was published, there were some unhappy *Ben's Chili Bowl* fans demanding to know why *Ben's* wasn't in the book. The answer, sheepishly, was this: I figured the decades-old, district institution spoke for itself—who hadn't been to *Ben's*? And then I started mulling it over, and the thought of someone visiting this town and not experiencing the original chili half-smoke was downright upsetting. What had I been thinking? I apologize profusely and can now promise that all you who read this book will now know of the best chili for miles.

imbibe / devour:
root beer
mellow yellow
ben's famous all-meat chili dog
ben's original chili half-smoke
chili con carne
chili-cheese fries
chocolate milk shake

biagio

fine chocolate shop

1904 18th street northwest. between t and u. red: dupont circle
202.328.1506 www.biagiochocolate.com
tue - sat noon - 8p sun noon - 5p

opened in 2007. owners: biagio abbatiello and william knight
$ - $$: all major credit cards accepted
treats. first come, first served

dupont circle > **e06**

There is a place in Manhattan that sells naps. Yes—in the middle of Gotham, in the middle of the day, you can buy a nap. In DC, if you're feeling sluggish and in need of a mid-day snooze, I suggest *Biagio*, where the regenerative cocoa bean reigns supreme. Here you'll find chocolate in many fine forms and sometimes interestingly paired with ingredients like ginger or pop rocks or spicy almonds or salt—the list goes on and on. *Biagio's* collection of chocolates are so beautiful, it's sometimes hard to eat them, but you'll get over that quickly. I'd much rather buy chocolates than naps.

imbibe / devour:
j. chocolatier truffles:
   sesame
   warm clove truffle
   fleur de sel caramel
k. chocolat chili almonds
stainer peperoncino italiano bar
pralus dark chocolate
artisan confections

big bear cafe

beloved coffee house

1700 first street northwest. corner of r
green: shaw-howard university
www.bigbearcafe-dc.com
mon - fri 7a - 8p sat 7:30 - 6p sun 8:30a - 6p

opened in 2006. owners: stu davenport and lana labermeier
$ - $$: all major credit cards accepted
breakfast. lunch. first come, first served

shaw district > **e07**

I think that at least half of the pleasure of a cup of fresh, black coffee has to do with the method in which it was brewed. If coffee in the morning meant simply pouring from a pot, sans prep, it wouldn't hold the same appeal. I alternate between three methods of brewing in my home—a classic drip machine, a Chemex glass coffee maker and a French press—with the last method being my favorite. This is why I love sitting in the brilliantly sunny *Big Bear*, watching as the Counter Culture coffee is prepared batch by batch by an army of French presses. The smell is divine. The brew perfection.

imbibe / devour:
macchiato
cappuccino
single-origin coffee brewed with a french press
breakfast sandwich
granola with milk or yogurt
turkey apple brie panino
roasted red pepper & tomato soup

bistro d'oc

languedoc cuisine from the south of france

518 tenth street northwest. between e and f. red / blue / orange: metro center
202.393.5444 www.bistrodoc.com
brunch sun 11:30a - 4p lunch mon - sat 11:30a - 2:30p t heatre daily 5:30 - 7p, 9 - 10p
dinner mon - thu 5:30 - 10p fri - sat 5:30 - 11p sun 4 - 8:30p

opened in 2002. chef / owner: bernard grenier
$$: all major credit cards accepted
brunch. lunch. dinner. pre and post theatre. reservations recommended

national mall > e08

One cold week in late January, I was on the hunt for an amazing bowl of french onion soup—is anything more soul-warming in the winter? It became a bit of a goldilocks hunt: one soup didn't have enough onions, another had too much cheese, another not quite the right cheese, another, too weak a broth. The day that I entered *Bistro D'oc*, I had a feeling my search had ended. As the perfect bowl of soup was placed in front of me, I could smell its just-rightness. Yes, this was the bowl. And loads better than porridge, that's for certain.

imbibe / devour:
03 sancerre coteaux fruite, loire valley
92 opus one, napa
onion soup gratinée
roasted p.e.i. mussels with garlic
hot ham & cheese croissant
white bean stew with duck, lamb, pork & sausage
grilled colorado lamb top sirloin
l'assiette de fromages

black salt

fish market and restaurant

4883 macarthur boulevard northwest. between u and v
202.342.9101 www.blacksaltrestaurant.com
brunch sun 11a - 2p lunch mon - sat 11:30a - 2:30p
dinner mon - thu 5:30 - 9:30p fri 5:30 - 11p sat 5 - 11p sun 5 - 9p fish market

opened in 2004. owners: jeff and barbara black   executive chef: jeff black
chef de cuisine: danny wells fishmonger: scott weinstein
$$ - $$$: all major credit cards accepted
brunch. lunch. dinner. reservations recommended

glover park > **e09**

Recently my dad and I were talking about salt. Table salt, kosher salt, sel du fleur, hawaiian red salt—the list is long. This chat got me thinking about *Black Salt*—the restaurant (and fish market), not the mineral—and how amazing it is that a piece of fish can taste so amazing, like something you've never eaten before. This is the experience you'll have at *Black Salt*. What makes the difference here, is the super-fresh, sustainably harvested seafood and the chefs simple, yet perfectly executed dishes. Once you've dined at *Black Salt*, you may never go back—to table salt or to any old humdrum fish.

imbibe / devour:
small production, artisan beers & wines
oysters on the half shell
fried rhode island calamari
crispy north carolina catfish sandwich
hard wood grilled loch duart salmon
whole mediterranean branzino
key lime pie
chocolate peanut butter crunch cake

buck's fishing & camping

american food that makes you proud to be an american

5031 connecticut avenue northwest. between huntington and harrison

red : tenleytown-au

202.364.0777

tue - sun 5 - 10p

opened in 2003. owner: james alefantis   chef / owner: carole greenwood

$$ - $$$: all major credit cards accepted

dinner. reservations recommended

On a high-school camping trip to Mount Jefferson in Oregon, I cooked my first meal in the great outdoors. I'm sorry to say I don't remember what I cooked, but I do remember my hands reeked of onions for days—the smell of the food lingering much longer than the taste—generally not the sign of a successful meal. At *Buck's Fishing & Camping*, you'll remember the taste of what you ate for days and days (and beyond) as Carole's classic American cuisine is truly memorable. This is my kind of fishing and camping.

imbibe / devour:
deviled organic eggs
the big camp salad
iceberg wedge with apple-wood smoked bacon
wood-grilled shrimp & grits with sausage
wood-grilled, dry-aged prime sirloin steak
hand-cut french fries
side of mac 'n' cheese
chocolate cake

café atlantico

nuevo latino cuisine

405 eighth street northwest. between d and e
green / yellow: archives-navy memorial
202.393.0812 www.cafeatlantico.com
brunch sat - sun 11:30a - 3:30p lunch tue - fri 11:30a - 2:30p
dinner tue - thu 5 - 10p fri - sat 5 - 11p sun 5 - 10p

opened in 1990. owners: rob wilder, josé andrés et al chef: katsuya fukushima
$$ - $$$: all major credit cards accepted
latino dim sum brunch. lunch. dinner. full bar. reservations recommended

penn quarter > **e11**

When my Dad found himself in DC recently, he needed a suggestion for a dining spot. *Café Atlantico* **came to mind immediately,** and I think it was the right suggestion. He called me at least twice throughout the meal to gush about the cozy table, the unbelievable cocktails, the food he and his dining companion stuffed themselves full with and the impeccable service. At the end of his meal, he said I must have called ahead to ensure they had an amazing experience. I assured him I had no such influence—this was simply the way it is for everyone who eats at *Café Atlantico*.

imbibe / devour:
mojito
pineapple caipirinha
grilled octopus with strawberries
dominican conch fritters
"organized" caesar salad
jerk chicken "mofongo"
sopa de mango

casa oaxaca

oaxacan cuisine

2106 18th street northwest. between california and wyoming. red: dupont circle
202.387.2272 www.oaxacaindc.com
tue - sat 5 - 11p sun 11a - 10p

opened in 2007. owners: karen barroso and rolando juarez chef: alfio blangiardo
$$: all major credit cards accepted
brunch. dinner. reservations recommended

adams morgan > **e12**

Browsing through this book, you'll find that there are several Mexican food spots, which DC has an amazing and varied selection of, so it was hard to pick favorites. *Casa Oaxaca* was an easy choice with its authentic Oaxacan cuisine, which is rooted in mole. If you are a lover of mole, you know that if you have one, you have *not* had them all. There are green, black, red, poblano moles and more. Some are heavier on the chocolate, some lighter, some are sweeter, some smokier. With its glorious menu of moles, *Casa Oaxaca* could well be called *Casa Mole*.

imbibe / devour:
top shelf margaritas
enmoladas
ravioli de huitlacoche
rellenitos de platano macho
mole negro oaxaqueño famosos tacos
mole verde con costillas de puerco
flan de horchata

cashion's eat place

upscale comfort food

1819 columbia road northwest. between biltmore and mintwood
red: woodley park-zoo / adams morgan
202.797.1819 www.cashionseatplace.com
tue 5:30 - 10p wed - sat 5:30 - 11p sun 11:30a - 2:30p 5:30 - 10p
fri - sat after dark menu midnight – 2am

opened in 1995. owners: justin abad, george manolatos and john manolatos
chef: john manolatos
$$ - $$$: all major credit cards accepted
brunch. dinner. reservations recommended

adams morgan > **e13**

Cashion's is legendary in this city. So when Ann Cashion sold the restaurant, there was a great to-do as loyalists got all in a tizzy about the place changing. Listen, I'm not a big fan of change either, but believe me, even without Ann—*Cashion's* is still downright outstanding. Outstanding brunch, outstanding dinner and an outstanding late-night menu that starts at midnight on weekends, an Adams Morgan experience not to be missed. In other words, *Cashion's* is forever outstanding.

imbibe / devour:
lamb keftedes with tomato, yogurt & dill
wild mushrooms with liver sauce over polenta
local turnip & ham soup
herb-marinated, new-frontier bison ribeye
brined organic chicken with mashed potatoes
crater lake blue cheese
grayson cheese

comet ping pong

ping pong and pizza

5037 connecticut avenue northwest. between huntington and harrison

red: tenleytown-au

202.364.0404

tue - fri 5 - 10p sat 11:30a - 10:30p sun 11:30a - 10p

opened in 2006. owner: james alefantis owner / chef: carole greenwood

$$: all major credit cards accepted

lunch. dinner. first come, first served

northwest >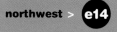

All those who went to *Chuck E. Cheese* when you were little, raise your hand. All those who have any interest in going there ever again, raise your hand. Right. Not so many hands in that second round. In theory, the idea is great, but for the adults, it can be a nightmare. For a totally opposite experience that is just as exciting to kids, head to *Comet Ping Pong*. Adults and kids alike can duel at the ping pong tables in back, and all ages will love Carole's pizzas, made with farm-fresh ingredients. Food has never been so fun.

imbibe / devour:
victory prima pils
caesar salad
pizzas:
  ace
  yalie
  steel wills
comet hot wings
tin roof sundae

dolcezza

artisanal gelato and sorbetto
1560 wisconsin avenue northwest. between q and p
blue / orange: foggy bottom-gwu
202.333.4646 www.dolcezzagelato.com
sun - thu 11a - 10p fri - sat 11a - midnight
see website for second location in bethesda

opened in 2006. owners: robb duncan, violeta edelman and dimas rodriguez
$: all major credit cards accepted
treats. first come, first served

georgetown > **e15**

Milk from grass-fed Jersey cows, hand-picked blackberries from local farms, and fresh market ingredients—it's hard to find a gelateria that takes its craft more seriously. *Dolcezza* is *the* place to get the creamiest, freshest and most innovative gelato in town, which is why I sat on the bench outside here for three days in a row, waiting for the doors to open. Three days in a row, you ask? Coincidentally, I happened to be in the area on all three days (really! Okay, not really), and you couldn't expect me to pass *Dolcezza* without stopping in. I bet you couldn't!

imbibe / devour:
gelati:
  sicilian blood orange
  grapefruit con campari
  meyer lemon
  dulce de leche classico
  ceylon cinnamon
  apple-cider clove
  chocolate classic

eamonn's

a dublin chipper

728 king street. corner of washington. blue / yellow : king street
703.299.8384 www.eamonnsdublinchipper.com
mon - wed 11:30a - 10p thu 11:30a - 11p fri 11:30a - midnight
sat noon - midnight sun noon - 10p

opened in 2006. owners: cathal and meshelle armstrong and todd thrasher
chef: cathal armstrong
$: all major credit cards accepted
lunch. dinner. first come, first served

alexandria > **e16**

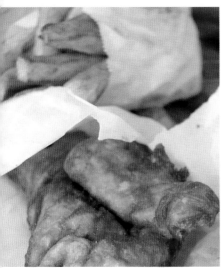

Snow White and the Seven Dwarfs. The seven natural wonders of the world. The seven deadly sins. I have yet another set of seven to add to the annals: the seven secret sauces at *Eamonn's*. They're every bit as diverse as the dwarfs, as wondrous as the wonders, and as deadly as the sins... in the best of ways, of course. I'm torn between the hot chili and the classic tartar for my fish, and I like to dunk my chips in the hot curry. Fish and chips, fried bananas, dough balls and seven sauces... I think I know which of the seven deadly sins I'm guilty of after a hearty trip to *Eamonn's*.

imbibe / devour:
guinness draft
fish & chips:
  cod
  ray
  prawns
dough balls
fried bananas
seven secret sauces

equinox

regional, seasonal, exceptional food

818 connecticut avenue northwest. between h and i. blue / orange : farragut west

202.331.8118 www.equinoxrestaurant.com

lunch mon - fri 11:30a - 2p

dinner mon - thu 5:30 - 10p fri - sat 5:30 - 10:30p sun 5 - 9p

opened in 1999. owners: todd and ellen gray chef: todd gray

$$$: all major credit cards accepted

lunch. dinner. reservations recommended

national mall > **e17**

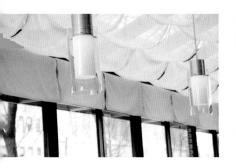

On a recent trip to New Orleans, I found myself engaging in the mandatory experience of eating beignets at *Café du Monde*. I noticed that at nearly every table, someone was snapping a photo, and it made me think of *Equinox*. While I was shooting here, I listened in on happy diners as they raved about the beauty of their meals. This is the kind of place that makes you want to take a picture of every dish and drink, so as to set it in your memory. Were they as equipped as the Nola tourists, I believe that *Equinox's* diners would have been snapping shots of every course.

imbibe / devour:
04 stuhlmuller cabernet sauvignon
pan-roasted maine diver scallops
sautéed jumbo-lump crab cakes
grilled loin of hawaiian blue marlin
sauteed strip loin of grass-fed veal
baked, truffled mac 'n' cheese
equinox risotto fritters
classic baba au rhum

georgetown cupcake

worth lining up for cupcakes

1209 potomac street northwest. between m and n
blue / orange: foggy bottom / gwu
202.333.8448 www.georgetowncupcake.com
tue - fri 11a - 7p sat 11a - 9p sun noon - 5p

opened in 2008. owners: katherine kallinis and sophie lamontagne
$: all major credit cards accepted
cupcakes. first come, first served

georgetown > e18

The first time I came to *Georgetown Cupcake*, it was before opening hours, and a few people lingered outside. I figured I'd stop by later. When I came back, it was open, with a line stretched out in front. No time to wait, I'd have to return. The third time, I again found a queue of fanatic cupcake eaters. The fourth time, I arrived just before closing, and they were cleaned out... not a cupcake left! When I finally tried one of the cupcakes, I discovered the secret—shockingly good frosting. These cupcakes are worth waiting for. The only trick is to get in line early enough before they sell out.

imbibe / devour:
cupcakes:
  red velvet
  lava fudge
  chocolate coconut
  chocolate peanut butter swirl
  vanilla & chocolate
  sunshine
  baby blue

grape + bean

wine, coffee and more

118 south royal street. between king and prince. blue / yellow: king street
703.664.0214 www.grapeandbean.com
check website for hours

opened in 2008. owners: david gwathmey and sheera rosenfeld
$ - $$: all major credit cards accepted
wine. coffee. snacks. first come, first served

alexandria >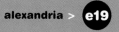

Everyone gets hit once in a while with a fit of procrastination. I, in a valiant effort to delay writing this book, just this morning created a dewey decimal-esque system for my spices. At times like this, the best thing is to just take the day off and make a trip to *Grape + Bean* because I figure either wine or coffee (or both!) will cure stubborn procrastination. A single brewed cup of exceptional coffee with a piece of dark, locally made chocolate—or a glass of wine and bite of cheese with freshly baked bread—these are things that are capable of giving me a fresh outlook. Now, back to work!

imbibe / devour:
coffee:
   dolok sanggul, sumatra
   gatuiri lot 4486, kenya
   la golondrina microlot, columbia
kingsbury chocolate
wines by small producers
restaurant eve's bread
cheeses, cheese boards & cheese knives

hank's oyster bar

fanastic oyster bar and local favorite

dupont: 1624 q street northwest. between 16th and 17th. red: dupont circle
alexandria: 1026 king street. between henry and patrick. yellow: king street
d: 202.462.4265 / a: 703.739.4265 www.hanksdc.com
see website for hours

opened in 2005. owner / chef : jamie leeds owner: sandy lewis
$$: all major credit cards accepted
brunch. lunch. dinner. first come, first served

dupont circle / alexandria >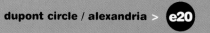

Is there anything in the world more glorious than having an enormous tray of oysters on the half-shell, sitting on their bed of crushed ice, ready to be devoured? It makes me feel like no matter where I am or what I'm doing, I'm on vacation. *Hank's Oyster Bar*—both the original locale and the newer Alexandria spot—is such a chill hangout spot to enjoy delicious seafood and a glass or two of something refreshing—it's like having a bit of r & r. So whether you're a visitor or a native, take yourself on a little vacay to *Hank's*.

imbibe / devour:
yuengling lager
brooklyn brown ale
oysters & clams on the half-shell
new england style clam chowder
oyster po' boy with cole slaw
fried oysters
lobster bisque

hook

sustainable seafood

3241 m street northwest. between wisconsin and potomac.
blue / orange: foggy bottom / gwu
202.625.4488 www.hookdc.com
brunch sat - sun 11a - 2p lunch mon - fri 11:30a - 2:30p
dinner sun - tue 5 - 10p wed - sat 5p - 11p

opened in 2007. owner: pure hospitality chef: joshua whigham
$$ - $$$: all major credit cards accepted
brunch. lunch. dinner. full bar. reservations recommended

georgetown > e21

Living in a sustainable way is easier than ever. It no longer means having to sacrifice style or comfort or really much of anything. In fact, it's becoming more common that organic, sustainable, eco choices are the more appealing ones in the end. *Hook* is a prime example: an exquisite restaurant in the middle of Georgetown, with a tasty menu that uses responsibly sourced seafood. Turns out, doing good makes things taste even better, and chances are that this place will have you sold in no time—hook, line and sinker. (How could I resist?)

imbibe / devour:
rosemary cocktail
byzantine cocktail
grilled calamari
steelhead tartar
black risotto
sablefish with almond milk & root vegetables
bluefish with potato-zucchini cake
yellowfin tuna with herbed potatoes

komi

modern american prix fixe

1509 17th street northwest. between p and q
red: dupont circle
202.332.9200 www.komirestaurant.com
tue - sat 5:30p - close

opened in 2004. owner / chef: johnny monis
$$ - $$$: all major credit cards accepted
dinner. reservations recommended

logan circle > e22

I spend a lot of time reading food reviews. I read what both the professionals and the amateurs have to say. I figure the extremes cancel each other out, and what is left is a distilled-down assessment culled from a group of diverse experiences: the wisdom of the crowd. So what I found remarkable, having read hundreds of reviews, is that appraisals of *Komi's* are over-the-top positive. Everyone loves Johnny's food, and this place gives a big impression. Whether from last week, or two years ago, the raves continue. The crowds are correct... this place rocks, one hundred percent.

imbibe / devour:
crudo of lobster with blood orange & chive
handmade spaghetti with catalina sea urchin,
   crab & habanero
tagliatelle with sweetbreads, snails & chanterelles
red beet vaiolini with feta & maple syrup
monkfish roasted on the bone
roasted suckling pig

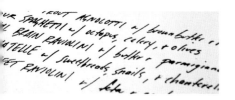

47

locanda

pasta better than your italian grandmother's

633 pennsylvania avenue southeast. blue / orange: eastern market
202.547.0002 www.locandadc.com
see website for hours

opened in 2007. chef: alonzo zoeller
$$: all major credit cards accepted
brunch. lunch. dinner. reservations recommended

capitol hill > **e23**

When I lived in Rome, I woke to the aroma of fresh basil and tomatoes coming from the street vendor selling fresh produce below my window. On my morning walk, I would stop at the same bar for my daily espresso where I was greeted by an always-friendly barista. For lunch, I'd go around the corner to a small trattoria where the handmade pasta changed every day. Take all of these things, mix them together, and you have *Locanda*. The homemade pasta is peerless, the staff is charming, and the place is intimate. I can't imagine a better trio for a superb Italian meal.

imbibe / devour:
04 barbera d'alba tre vigne
burrata & prosciutto di parma
maccheroncelli
pasta al frutti di mare
porcini gnocchi
chianti-braised lamb shank
grilled whole branzino
pistacchio gelato & cookies

mandu

traditional korean cuisine

1805 18th street northwest. between s and t. red: dupont circle
202.588.1540 www.mandudc.com
mon - thu 11a - 10p fri - sat 11:30a - 11p sun 11:30a - 9p

opened in 2006. owners: yesoon lee and danny lee chef: yesoon lee
$$: all major credit cards accepted
brunch. lunch. dinner. happy hour. first come, first served

dupont circle > e24

At *Mandu*, Yesoon is making homemade, authentic Korean food that you won't find anywhere else in the city. Friends, forget all of the detox diets out there, forget the cleansing fasts and concoctions designed to "center" you. All you need is the steaming-hot-to-the-last-bite bibim bap here. This dish will bring you all the clarity you need and heal you inside and out. It is soul-warming, home-cooked food that will make you wish Yesoon were your own mother; alas, she is not. But you can (and should) come and eat her food any day of the week.

imbibe / devour:
grape sojutini
mandu dumplings
pan-fried eggplant
kalbi-tang soup
bibim bap
kalbi-marinated short ribs
dak jeem chicken
green tea ice cream

mixtec

cheerful café serving regional mexican food

1792 columbia road northwest. corner of 18th street
red: woodley park-zoo / adams morgan
202.332.1011 www.mixtecdc.com
sun - thu 10a - 10p fri - sat 10a - 11p

opened in 1981. owner: pepe montesinos
$ - $$: all major credit cards accepted
breakfast. brunch. lunch. dinner. first come, first served

adams morgan > **e25**

I don't know what it is, but every time I find myself at *Mixtec*, I am escaping from a torrential downpour. It's as though the heavens themselves are leading me to this glorious little Mexican haven. I usually come dripping wet into this bright restaurant, and I never want to leave—stuffing myself with tacos and sipping margaritas like it's my last day on earth. On the gloomiest of days, *Mixtec* will make you feel like everything is brilliant again. It's a spicy antidote to winter woes and bad-day blues. You'll be ready to brave the storms after your sojourn here.

imbibe / devour:
sangria
modelo especial
café con leche
camarones acapulco
enchiladas de fiesta
tacos al carbon
guacamole
arroz con leche

oyamel

cochina mexicana

401 seventh street northwest. corner of d. green / yellow: archives-navy memorial
202.628.1005 www.oyamel.com
sun - mon 11:30a - 10p tue - thu 11:30a - 11:30p fri - sat 11:30a - midnight
brunch sat - sun 11:30a - 3p

opened in 2007. owners: think food group. chef: joe raffa
$$: all major credit cards accepted
brunch. lunch. dinner. reservations recommended

penn quarter >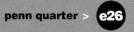

I really enjoy a meal that is prepared tableside. You know, shaken margaritas poured into your glass upon arrival or even tableside fish deboning. At the top of this list is tableside mashed guacamole. The cartful of equipment and voluptuous avocados, the scooping and squeezing and smashing—the anticipation is downright exhilarating! As you can imagine, the guacamole here at *Oyamel* does not disappoint in show or in flavor. The only real problem I face is filling up on chips and guac before the equally tasty tacos arrive. Not a bad problem to have.

imbibe / devour:
pineapple margarita
tamarind tea
guacamole al tomatillo con queso fresco
enchilada de pollo con salsa verde
tinga poblana taco
tacos de hongos
cochinita pibil con cebolla en escabeche tacos
cajeta tradicional y moderna

proof

wine-centric restaurant

775 g street nw. between seventh and eighth
green / red / yellow: gallery place-chinatown 202.737.7663 www.proofdc.com
lunch mon - fri 11:30a - 2p
dinner mon - wed 5:30 - 10p thu - sat 5:30 - 11p sun 5 - 9:30p
bar mon - wed 5:30p - 1a thu - sat 5:30p - 2a sun 5p - midnight

opened in 2007. owner: mark kuller chef: haidar karoum
$$ - $$$: all major credit cards accepted
lunch. dinner. full bar. reservations recommended

penn quarter > **e27**

"Wine is constant proof that god loves us and loves to see us happy," said Benjamin Franklin. If this founding father believed this to be true (judging from his curriculum vitae, he's the one brain I might tend to listen to), then what more reason do you need to come to *Proof* to enjoy their enormous wine list? You'll need the rest of your days to explore and taste all of the proof here, so you should start soon. Pair the grape with food from the organically driven menu, and you will have found a virtual Garden of Eden in downtown DC. You'll never feel so loved and enlightened as after a stop here.

imbibe / devour:
65 pages of wine
chef's full charcuterie board
beautiful array of cheese
prosciutto & fresh ricotta piadina
ahi tuna tartare with nori tempura
braised little meatballs
yukon gold gnocchi
foie gras scrambled eggs

px

speakeasy lounge featuring handcrafted cocktails
728 king street. look for the blue light. blue / yellow: king street
703.~~200~~.8384 www.eamonnsdublinchipper.com
_299_
wed - sat 7p - close

opened in 2006. owners: cathal and meshelle armstrong and todd thrasher
drink maker: todd thrasher
$$: all major credit cards accepted
full bar. reservations recommended

alexandria > **e28**

Something has happened to cocktails in this country—somehow we got lazy about them. Bottled soda water, pre-made mixes, unimaginative combos. I guess the thinking was who can top the classic gin and tonic? So we stopped trying. Until now. Call it the cocktail comeback, the revival of the real mixed drink—Todd with his concoctions at *PX* is leading the pack. Housemade bitters, hand-squeezed juices, freshly brewed tonic and never-before-seen creations that make me realize what I've been missing all of these years. This is one speakeasy you won't want to speak softly about.

imbibe / devour:
cocktails:
  eamonn's
  dan's father's pisco sour
  my wife's manhattan
  grog, master henry morgan
  pawpaw
  the sherlock holmes
  china rose

restaurant eve

historic dining in a historic building

110 south pitt street. corner of king. blue / yellow : king street
703.706.0450 www.restauranteve.com
lunch mon - fri 11:30a - 2:30p dinner mon - sat 5:30 - 10p
tasting room dinner mon - sat 5:30 - 9:30p

opened in 2004. owners: catal and meshelle armstrong chef: cathal armstrong
$$$: all major credit cards accepted
lunch. dinner. full bar. reservations recommended

alexandria >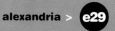

Sometimes I wonder what it would be like if we all still lived in the Garden of Eden, had Eve not bollixed it up with the apple. I think the food there couldn't be too far off from what *Restaurant Eve* creates, where the ingredients don't travel far from the earth to your plate. Cathal's menu is sourced from local farmers, and Eden-worthy items like morels, baby white asparagus and truffles show up often. With an outdoor verandah, and a warm and welcoming interior, it's hard to imagine a more heavenly setting. This place was named after Cathal's daughter, Eve, and what a true paradise it is.

imbibe / devour:
jefferson's crimson
black currant fizz
housemade charcuterie
housemade lemon & lobster ravioli
muscovy duck leg confit with du puy lentils
bouillabaisse—saffron jus with cod, clams & rouille
toffee sticky buns with apple cider sauce

rice

shockingly delicious thai food

1608 14th street northwest. between q and r
green: u street / african american civil war memorial / cardozo
202.234.2400 www.ricerestaurant.com
lunch mon - thu 11a - 2:30p
dinner mon - thu 5 - 10:30p fri - sat 11a - 11p sun 11a - 10:30p

opened in 2003. owner: sak pollert chef: phannarai promprasert
$$: all major credit cards accepted
lunch. dinner. full bar. first come, first served

14th street >

I've found that there are generally two types of travelers: those who plan like crazy, and those who just explore. I fall into the former category, obsessively mapping out everything, with multiple meal options broken down by neighborhood. If you're anything like I am, and you're reading through this book fretting about where to eat first, I'll make things easier for you: go to *Rice*. No matter what, put it on your schedule. Whether for lunch or dinner—you have my word, you won't be disappointed. Even you non-planners out there will want to plan on this one.

imbibe / devour:
singha beer
mai tai
papaya salad with shrimp
shrimp salad with crispy coconut & grapefruit
tom kha gai soup
green curry chicken with thai eggplant & basil
pad thai with chicken
fried chicken with crispy lemongrass

simply home

world cuisine with thai flavor

1410 u street northwest. between 14th and 15th
green: u street / african-american civil war memorial / cardozo
202.232.8424 www.simplyhomedc.com
daily 11:30a - 11p

opened in 2006. owners: sak pollert, mike weber and friends
chef: phannarai promprasert
$$: all major credit cards accepted
lunch. dinner. brunch. full bar. happy hour. first come, first served

u street > **e31**

On my last day of shooting, eating, and trekking all across the city working on this book, I gave myself a reward. Not a hot bath, pedicure and a liquid diet—instead, I treated myself to my very favorite meal in the city: dinner at *Simply Home*. DC is full of incredible eats, but nothing compares to the fresh and spicy goodness that comes out of *Simply Home's* kitchen. Every time I eat here, I am truly fulfilled. I make it my mission to clean every plate, down to the very last bite of mango and sticky rice.

imbibe / devour:
harushika sake
seafood apple salad with ginger dressing
fresh garden roll
pineapple fried rice
burmese kao soi noodles with shrimp
sautéed chicken with asian pumpkin & basil
panang shrimp tempura
sticky rice with mango

sonoma

cozy restaurant and wine bar

223 pennsylvania avenue southeast. between second and third
orange / blue: capitol south
202.544.8088 www.sonomadc.com
lunch mon - fri 11:30a - 2:30p
dinner mon - thu 5:30 - 10p fri - sat 5:30 - 11p sun 5:30 - 9p

opened in 2005. owners: elias hengst and jared rager chef: drew trautman
$$ - $$$: all major credit cards accepted
lunch. dinner. full bar. reservations recommended

capitol hill > **e32**

Every now and then, I toy with the idea of vegetarianism. There isn't a vegetable I've met that isn't my friend and I think tofu can be tasty and I can even go for a week without eating animals. And then reality hits—I would have to give up the charcuterie board at *Sonoma*. I think of the oh-so-lovely cured meats on it and good intentions go out the window. I also think of *Sonoma's* wine list, and how tofu never did anything for a glass of wine. Nope, meat glorious meat—and glorious wine for that matter—are for me!

imbibe / devour:
05 elyse nero misto
06 cobblestone napa valley rosé
my beloved charcuterie board
honey-glazed quail
wild mushroom farrotto
shenandoah lamb ragnoma hash
whole roasted local porgy
create your own pizzas

sticky fingers bakery

a vegan bakery

1370 park road northwest. between 13th and 14th. green: columbia heights
202.299.9700 www.stickyfingersbakery.com
mon - thu 7a - 7p fri 7a - 9p sat 8a - 9p sun 9a - 5p

opened in 2001. owners: kirsten rosenberg and doron greenblatt petersan
$: all major credit cards accepted
treats. first come, first served

columbia heights >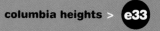

I am convinced that the bakers at *Sticky Fingers* are real-life magicians. How do they do it? They remove from their sweet treats eggs, dairy and all the fats and oils that are bad for us but make things taste good. By my logic (or if I was the baker) you'd end up with flavorless, cardboard-y, baked goods. Not so. It's magic! The cream-filled oatmeal sandwich and oreo-esque cookies and chocolate cupcakes are ridiculously tasty, making me crave these and all the delights here much more than their unhealthy relatives. This truly is magic!

imbibe / devour:
direct trade coffee
chocolate chimp bread
sticky cinnamon buns
cowvin cookies
old-fashioned chocolate chip cookies
little devils
peanut butter fudge cake
s'mores cupcakes

tabard inn

cozy restaurant at the inn

1739 north street northwest. between 17th and 18th. red: dupont circle
202.331.8528 www.tabardinn.com
breakfast mon - fri 7 - 10a sat 8 - 9:45a sun 8 - 9:15a
brunch sat 11a - 2:30p sun 10:30a - 2p lunch mon - fri 11:30a - 2:30p
dinner sun - thu 6 - 9:30p fri - sat 6 - 10p

opened in 1975. owner: jeremiah cohen chef: paul pelt
$$: all major credit cards accepted
brunch. lunch. dinner. full bar. reservations recommended

dupont circle > e34

Ever since I read *A Room with a View*, I've been longing to travel in the way of the early 20th-century English, where guests come to the dining room of the villa where they're staying and dine with the same quirky fellow guests day after day. Cozy *Tabard Inn* makes me feel like I am Miss Lucy Honeychurch herself on a romantic travel adventure, starting my day with a sensible, home-cooked breakfast. Then there's the not-so-sensible weekend brunch with housemade fried donuts and desserts like gorgonzola cheesecake—as rich as the romance between Forester's Mr. Emerson and Miss Lucy.

imbibe / devour:
hot coffee
tabard's own freshly fried donuts
toasted pecan waffles
old-fashioned oatmeal
apple sticky toffee pudding cake
applewood smoked bacon
island creek oysters
medjool date & pip dreams goat-cheese salad

taqueria distrito federal

authentic mexican taqueria
3463 14th street northwest. corner of oak street. green: columbia heights
202.276.7331
mon - wed 7a - 10p thu - sat 6a - midnight

opened in 2005. owner: luis marroquin
$: cash
breakfast. lunch. dinner. first come, first served

columbia heights > **e35**

Stuck in California's terrible Napa Valley traffic, my husband and I pulled into a nondescript Mexican grocery on the side of the road. Inside, we found a back counter where they were handmaking hot, fresh tacos, then wrapping them in foil. We took ours out back to eat on the picnic bench and loved them so much, we went back for more. Since then, we both have had lusty desires for those tacos but hadn't found any that came close. That is, until I had *Distrito Federal's* tacos. These fill me with the same desire. I want to eat them until I burst with pleasure.

imbibe / devour:
horchata
tacos:
  al pastor
  carnitas
  al pollo
chorizo tostada
carne asada torta
menudo

TAQUERIA
TAQUERIA
STRITO FEDERAL
RESTAURANT

73

taqueria nacional

take-out tacos

400 north capitol street northwest. between louisiana and e. red: union station
202.737.7070 www.taquerianational.com
mon - fri 7a - 3p

opened in 2007. owners: ann cashion and john fulchino
$ - $$: all major credit cards accepted
breakfast. lunch. first come, first served

capitol hill > e36

I'm a snob about fast food. I've avoided the stuff for most of my life and hadn't even tried a hamburger from the golden arches until a couple of years ago when a friend convinced me I could barely call myself a U.S. citizen until I had. But *Taqueria Nacional* has the kind of fast food I can embrace because even though it gets to me quickly, it's still carefully crafted and created. From the succulent pulled-pork tacos to the tasty Spanish rice and fresh-made aguas, everything is made with freshest produce and meats. Slow food made fast, for all the world to enjoy. Yum.

imbibe / devour:
aguas frescas
guacamole & chips
tacos:
  egg & cheese
  chorizo & cheese
  pork tacos
spanish rice
yucca fries

teaism

a tea house and restaurant

800 connecticut avenue northwest. between 17th and connecticut
blue / orange: farragut west
202.835-2233 www.teaism.com
see website for addresses for other two locations and hours

opened in 1996. owners: michelle brown and linda neumann
$$: all major credit cards accepted
breakfast. brunch. lunch. dinner. first come, first served

national mall / penn quarter / dupont circle > e37

There are three locations of *Teaism* (two tea houses and the third a tea house/shop which you can read about on page 163) in DC. This means that wherever I am in this town, I'm bound to be near a *Teaism*—which means I have to use all of my will power to *not* go in and get a salty oat cookie. If you've ever tasted this scrumptious morsel, you know why my will failed me every time I passed by. This cookie is addictive. So next time you stop in for a perfect cup of tea here, I dare you to resist. Nothing is better than tea and cookies, and this is as true as ever when that cookie is a salty oat one.

imbibe / devour:
teas:
   jinzhen black
   jasmine pearl green
   tie guanyin oolong
bento boxes
plum ochazuke
salty oat cookie
jasmine crème brûlée

the majestic

royal, american classics

911 king street. between alfred and patrick. blue and yellow: king street
703.837.9117 www.majesticcafe.com
lunch mon - sat 11:30a - 2:30p
dinner mon - thu 5:30 - 10p fri - sat 5:30 - 10:30p sun 1 - 9p

opened in 1932. owners: cathal and meshelle armstrong and todd thrasher
chef: shannon "red" overmiller
$: all major credit cards accepted
lunch. dinner. first come, first served

alexandria > **e38**

Once upon a time, there was a place in Old Town called *The Majestic Café*. It was outfitted with the most stylish of décor, and meals were served to adoring regulars. After many decades of service, it began to tarnish. Then along came Alexandria's Prince Cathal, who saved the landmark café from closing its doors, and soon revived it, serving classic American comfort food and cocktails. Cathal and Meshelle were crowned King and Queen, and everyone who ate the home-style meatloaf, fried green tomatoes and chocolate cake here lived happily ever after. The End.

imbibe / devour:
fried green tomatoes
home-style meatloaf
majestic chicken
nana's sunday dinner
chesapeake bay seafood stew
oyster po' boy
ice-box cakes
cookies & milk shake

vegetate

delicious vegetarian cuisine

1414 9th street northwest. between p and q
green / yellow: mount vernon square / 7th street convention center
202.232.4585 www.vegetatedc.com
tue - thu 6 - 10p fri 6 - 11p sat noon - 11p

opened in 2005. owners: dominic and jennifer redd
$$ - $$$: all major credit cards accepted
dinner. reservations recommended

shaw district > **e39**

At the beginning of his book *In Defense of Food*, Michael Pollan writes, "Eat food. Not too much. Mostly plants." There is no better place to make good on such a statement as *Vegetate*. The folks here work with local and family-run farms to get the freshest produce. In fact, just one meal at *Vegetate* could convince even the heartiest meat eater that the vegetable is mighty desirable. As for Pollan's counsel on not eating too much, all I have to say is good luck sticking to that advice when you're dining here.

imbibe / devour:
thai basil gimlet
green tea cool out
vegetate burgers
roasted spring onion soup
native harvest wild-rice cakes
wild mushroom flatbread
seasonal vegetable risotto
blue-cheese skilletcakes

• all of the businesses featured in this book are locally owned. in deciding the businesses to feature, we require this first and foremost. and then we look for businesses that strike us as utterly authentic, whether they be new or old, chic or funky. and since this is not an advertorial guide, businesses do not pay to be featured.

• explore from neighborhood to neighborhood. note that almost every neighborhood featured has dozens of great stores and restaurants other than our favorites listed in this book.

• the maps in this guide are not highly detailed but instead are representational of each area noted. we highly suggest, if you are visiting, to also have a more detailed map. streetwise maps are always a good bet, and are easy to fold up and take along with you.

• make sure to double check the hours of the business before you go by calling or visiting its website. often the businesses change their hours seasonally. also, businesses that are featured sometimes close — this is often the sobering reality for many small, local businesses.

• the pictures and descriptions of each business are representational. please don't be distraught when the business no longer carries or is not serving something you saw or read about in the guide.

• the *eat.shop* clan consists of a small crew of creative types who travel extensively and have dedicated themselves to great eating and interesting shopping around the world. each of these people writes, photographs and researches his or her own books, and though they sometimes do not live in the city of the book they author, they draw from a vast network of local sources to deepen the well of information used to create the guides.

• there are three ranges of prices noted for restaurants, $ = cheap, $$ = medium, $$$ = expensive

• if you own the previous edition of *eat.shop washington dc*, make sure to keep it. think of the each edition as part of an overall "volume" of books, as many of the businesses no longer featured are still open and still fantastic. and note, the reason businesses are no longer featured in the guide is not because we don't like them anymore, but because there are so many amazing businesses that need a chance to be featured. to see past businesses, go to our website where all editions are available in online or e-book format.

eat.shop.sleep

there are many great places to stay in dc, but here are a few of my picks:

hotel palomar
2121 p street northwest (dupont circle)
202.448.1800 / hotelpalomar-dc.com
standard double from $230
restaurant: urbana
notes: hotel with top-notch extras like an in-room yoga studio

hotel tabard inn
1739 n street northwest (dupont circle)
202.785.1277 / tabardinn.com
standard double from $160
restaurant: tabard inn
notes: cozy, character-filled inn with famed weekend brunch

park hyatt washington
24 and m streets northwest (near georgetown)
202.789.1234 / parkwashington.hyatt.com
standard double from $299
restaurant: blue duck tavern
lounge / bar: tea cellar
notes: luxe hotel with gorgeous dining options

sofitel
806 15th street northwest (lafayette square)
202.730.8800 / sofitel.com
standard double from $220
restaurant: ici urban bistro
bar: le bar
notes: comfort meets chic

• adams morgan

eat

e2 > amsterdam falafel shop
e12 > casa oaxaca
e13 > cashion's eat place
e25 > mixtec

shop

s1 > and beige
s23 > meeps
s37 > the brass knob

note: all maps face nor

willard st nw
t st nw
e6
t st nw
swann st nw
swan st nw
e24
s st nw
s st nw
16th st nw
20th st nw
19th st nw
riggs pl nw
new hampshire ave nw
17th st nw
riggs pl nw
s36
r st nw
r st nw
r st nw
connecticut ave nw
corcoran st nw
s34
e20
q st nw
q st nw
q st nw
18th st nw
church st nw
e22
p st nw
dupont cir nw
p st nw
p st nw
hopkins st
20th st nw
17th st
q st nw
massachusetts ave nw
s16
s43
new hampshire ave nw
16th st nw
e34
n st nw
n st nw
st matthews ct nw
18th st

u street
14th street

eat

e4 > bar pilar
e20 > hank's oyster bar
e22 > komi
e30 > rice
e31 > simply home

shop

s1 > and beige
s6 > caramel
s9 > circle boutique
s12 > garden district
s13 > go mama go
s14 > good wood
s15 > greater goods
s17 > home rule
s24 > miss pixie's furnishings & whatnot
s25 > muleh
s26 > nana
s27 > palace 5ive
s29 > pop
s30 > rckndy
s31 > redeem

and beige

beautiful, neutral-palette furniture and home décor

1781 florida avenue northwest. between vernon and california
red: dupont circle
202.234.1557 www.andbeige.com
tue - sat 11a - 7p sun noon - 6p mon by appointment only

opened in 2007. owner: daren miller
all major credit cards accepted

adams morgan > **s01**

In a high-school art class, a classmate told me that I didn't understand color, because I never wore it. Peers have teased me since about my single-shade style tendencies as I prefer to stick to the neutrals: beige, brown, black and gray. So you can imagine my joy at discovering *And Beige*, a store whose monochromatic aesthetic had me seeing colors. True, not everything in this whole store is beige, but it is the focus, with complements of black, brown and white playing supporting roles. It's good to know that Mies van der Rohe and I aren't the only ones who believe that less is indeed more.

covet:
insect prints
bronze vertebrae
natural, turned teak balls
cable-knitted pillows
hand-blown jars
faux bois table lamp
carved bone stick insect

apartment zero

modern design for urban living

406 seventh street northwest. corner of d
green / yellow: archives-navy memorial
202.628.4067 www.apartmentzero.com
wed - sat 11a - 6p sun noon - 5p

opened in 1999. owners: douglas burton and christopher ralston
all major credit cards accepted
online shopping (by email, fax or phone). wishlists. design services

penn quarter >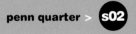

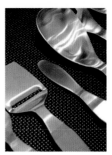

At first glance, *Apartment Zero* might seem out of place in a distinctly non-shopping district. But when you look around and see its neighbors—the National Gallery of American Art, the National Portrait Gallery and the National Gallery of Art—it makes sense that this distinctive store would be situated among notable art museums. Though the intention is to shop here, take note—you're bound to learn as much about modern design and designers as you would at any art museum. Consider it DC's MoMA, without the long lines to get in, and you get the opportunity to own the design icons on display.

covet:

walter gropius for rosenthal tac porcelain
collective tools bottle opener
frederickson stallard for citizen-citizen brush #2
touch wooden bench
oiva toikka for iittala queen red ibis bird
scott franklin for non design wet lamp
bensen pool table
india hazel linens

97

après peau

gifts and souvenirs from our nation's capital

1430 k street northwest. between vermont and 14th
blue / orange: mcpherson square
202.783.0022 www.aprespeau.com
mon - fri 10a - 6p

opened in 2001. owner: tina alster
all major credit cards accepted
online shopping (by phone). corporate gifts

national mall > **s03**

I love the idea of bringing home a souvenir to give as a gift from a trip. I do not love the idea that those souvenirs might be something like an "I Heart DC" tee or a White House snow globe. These gifts say, "I was at the airport and I forgot to get you something special." Plan ahead a bit, and stop into *Après Peau*, where you will find elegant, creative gifts ranging from custom-made, limited-edition chocolates to cufflinks made from authentic trolley tokens and letterpressed cards printed with words from past First Ladies' love letters. Special indeed.

covet:
signature stationery & chocolates
louise mathieson ceramics
miller et bertaux perfume
waals world clock
richartz pocket knife
lancome absolue
giorgio fedon orange keychain

bellacara

bath and beauty

924 king street. corner of patrick
blue / yellow: king street
703.299.9652 www.bellacara.com
mon - sat 11a - 6p sun noon - 5p

opened in 2000. owners: angela sitilides and kimberly putens
all major credit cards accepted
make-up/skincare events

alexandria >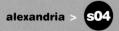

fresh.

MANGOSTEEN
BATH & SHOWER GEL

··· ✦ ···

WITH POMEGRANATE
EXTRACT

· ✦ ·

GEL MOUSSANT

· ✦ ·

300 ml ℮ 10 floz

When I was growing up, my mom and I would designate certain days beauty days. This didn't mean that we booked a full day of spa appointments, but instead we pulled out all of our beauty-making accoutrements and had a jam-packed DIY beauty day. To make a day like this at-home luxurious, you must be well supplied with products, and *Bellacara* is the perfect place to pick up prettifying items. They stock a varied and carefully chosen collection that will make you want to keep your beauty cupboards stocked.

covet:
kiehls lip gloss
paula dorf lipstick
susanne lang red ginger perfume
l'artisan parfumeur candles
fresh everything
sara happ brown sugar lip scrub
lippman collection nail polish
kiss me mascara

bobbie medlin

sacred objects as jewelry

1155 30th street northwest. between m and k
blue / orange: foggy bottom-gwu
202.333.2630 www.bobbiemedlin.com
wed - sun 11a - 6p

opened in 2005. owner: bobbie medlin
all major credit cards accepted

georgetown >

Ever since I met the wonderful Bobbie, I've been in awe of her way of life and her approach to her craft. Bobbie travels across the globe, where she has made connections with people in India, China, the Middle East and across Africa. Through these friendships, she has collected exquisite, one-of-a-kind relics and antiquities worthy of a place in a museum and crafted beautiful pieces of art out of them. Her eye is impeccable, her taste is bold, and her stories are fascinating. To be in this extraordinary woman's store is like visiting a foreign land filled with mystery and beauty.

covet:

necklaces:
  tibetan prayer box with turquoise beads
  turkoman protective silver amulet
  the melange series
  19th century rajasthani silver pendant
  indian rupee coins
  african bronze rings on silver braided chain
  19th century tibetan flint pouch with coral

caramel

clothing, art and accessories for men and women

1603 u street northwest. corner of 16th
green : u street / african-american civil war memorial / cardozo
202.265.1930 www.caramelfashion.com
thu - fri noon - 9p sat 11a - 7p sun noon - 5p

opened in 2006. owner: sarah watkins
mc. visa

u street >

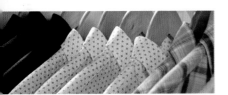

I've been reading about feng shui lately, specifically space clearing, energy fields and unblocking energy by arranging objects in our physical spaces. I realized it's a bit like doing an energy reading when I first enter a store—I feel vibes (good or bad) before I've seen anything or talked to anyone. When I walked into *Caramel*, I immediately felt positive energy, like everything was in the right place and in the right way. It lured me in, and once I saw the carefully arranged and well-edited duds for women and men, and met the lovely Sarah, I realized everything truly was in perfect harmony.

covet:
l-shandi dresses
fino handbags
alpana bawa shirts for men
panda snack bamboo t's
samunderneath everything
leather island belts
even keel yogawear

catharine roberts / oliver dunn / moss & co.

antiques for the home and garden

1657 wisconsin avenue northwest. corner of resevoir
orange and blue lines: foggy bottom-gwu
c. roberts / oliver dunn: 202.338.7410 m & co: 202.337.0540
tue - sat 11a - 5p

opened in 1993. owners: catharine roberts, moki heston and jackie oliver dunn
all major credit cards accepted

georgetown > 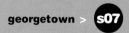 **s07**

Whenever I come into this store, I always remind myself of the saying, "a rolling stone gathers no moss." It's a funny thought to have in a place filled with antiques as it's just this type of stuff that should be gathering moss. But the ladies at *Catharine Roberts, Moss & Co.* and *Oliver Dunn* don't let their vintage beauties molder. Sourced from around the world, the antiques are ready for a new life and perfect to mix with contemporary styles. So the only moss you'll find here is in the sunny oasis in back.

covet:
antique:
  mercury glass candlesticks
  etched wine glasses
  meter stick
  birdcages
antheor dinnerware
nappe tablecloths
comptoir de famille linens

chinoiserie

eclectic finds from around the globe

1024 king street. between south henry and south patrick
blue / yellow: king street
703.838.0520
tue - sat 11a - 7p sun noon - 6p

opened in 2000. owner: peter zia
mc. visa

alexandria >

What a great suprise it was when I spied a box of Gwen Frostic cards at *Chinoiserie*. Gwen is well known to those of us who have spent a lifetime of summers in the Michigan woods, where her studio has been churning out woodsy prints on cards and paper napkins for eternity, but it was a thrilling anomaly to find the familiar cards in Alexandria. Peter manages to unearth the most eclectic, wonderful and obscure finds to fill his shop—from good-luck terra cotta pigs from Mexico to cigarette-thin lighters from Japan. *Chinoiserie* never disappoints, always charms, and sometimes even surprises.

covet:
three-legged "chanchitos" (good-luck pigs)
gwen frostic for roost note cards
heath ceramics
eau de yosh
mini piggy banks
glass beads
red hook & ladder fire truck

circle boutique

unfussy fashion for guys and girls

1736 14th street northwest. between r and s
green: u street / african-american civil war memorial / cardozo
202.518.2212 www.circleboutique.com
tue - fri noon - 7p sat 11a - 7p sun noon - 6p

opened in 2004. owners: dinah simpson, rosana vollmerhausen and wayne skinner
all major credit cards accepted
online shopping

14th street > **s09**

Lapping *Circle Boutique*, taking in their newish digs, I began to realize that it wasn't only their locale that had changed but also their evolving offerings. I began to get giddy, finding lines I'd never seen before as well as indie stalwarts I love. Somehow, in this small and understated space, they've managed to pull together an equal amount of great stuff for both girls and guys, which is unusual as guys tend to get short-changed when boutiques offer goods for both sexes. Now I'm just running around in circles trying to pick what I want for me and for my man.

covet:
chunky white saja sweater
lewis cho tunic
william rast jeans
mike & chris blue hooded zip-up
mike & chris t's for men
band of outsiders for men
king squire's den wool knit hat

coup de foudre

parisian inspired lingerie

1001 pennsylvania avenue northwest. corner of eleventh and e
red / blue / orange lines: metro center
202.393.0878 www.coupdefoudrelingerie.com
mon-sat 11a - 6p

opened in 2003. owners: valerie lucas and francoise david
all major credit cards accepted
online shopping. bra fitting. personal shopping

penn quarter >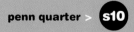

Ladies, listen up. Clean out your underwear drawer. Those ancient droopy drawers and dingy bras aren't doing anyone any favors, you least of all. The average underwear drawer could use spicing up—just the fact alone that I'm calling it an underwear drawer and not a lingerie drawer gives an idea about the general state of affairs. Follow my advice and head to *Coup de Foudre*. Valerie and her mother, Francoise, are experts and can outfit your underthings wardrobe with everything you need from basics to not-so-basics. Maybe then you can start referring to your lingerie drawer.

covet:
hanky panky anything
simone perele paradis bra
simone perele grenadines bustier
chantelle chantilly glamour bra
cosabella bikini underwear in multiple colors
cosabella valeria camisole
belabumbum mai tai bikini underwear

daniel donnelly

classic modern furniture and design

520 north fayette street. between pendleton and oronoco. blue / yellow : braddock road
703.549.4672 www.danieldonnelly.com
mon 11a - 6p thu - fri 11a - 6p sat noon - 6p sun noon - 5p
tue - wed by appointment

opened in 1986. owner: daniel donnelly and patricia clarkson
all major credit cards accepted
custom orders / design

alexandria > 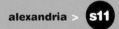 **s11**

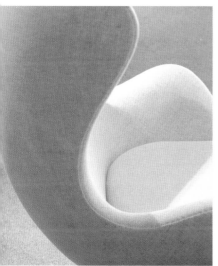

Daniel Donnelly is brilliant. Have you ever seen a piece of vintage mid-century furniture that you love, but it needs a bit of help? For example, the color of wood used in the piece doesn't quite fit with your current décor or a couch that has lost its springiness? The design studio here has a solution. Show them the piece and share with them your needs, and they'll recreate a custom version for you. Perfect. Or if you're just shopping, not only do they have new classics designed in-house, but they also have a who's who of pieces from the modern masters.

covet:
daniel donnelly low box on legs
daniel donnelly 4907 sofa group
machine age torch lamp
ray eames time life stools
bruno mathsson pernilla chair
george nelson marshmallow sofa
finn juhl design chieftain chair
herman miller picnic posters

garden district

an urban garden shop

exterior shop: 1801 14th street northwest. corner of s
interior shop: 1520 14th street northwest. corner of church
green: u street / african-american civil war memorial / cardozo
202.797.9005 www.gardendistrict-dc.com
see website for hours

opened in 2002. owner: joe carmack
all major credit cards accepted

14th street >

Spring is a magical thing. For months and months we hibernate, groaning through the conditions of winter (wet rain, hail, sleet and snow for example), longing for warmth, sun and spring flowers. Then one fine day, spring arrives as though it never left, starting with a budding bloom on a branch. This is the time when *Garden District* blooms as well and reopens its exterior shop. But this year you won't have to check days off the calendar waiting to shop at *Garden District*. Instead, you can head to the new interior shop, which is open year round, making the cold days just a little warmer.

covet:
potted herbs
bamboo
clematis
lady fern
wisteria
narcissus
christmas trees
landscaping supplies

go mama go!

multicultural home, tabletop and party décor store

1809 14th street northwest. between s and t
green: u street / african-american civil war memorial / cardozo
202.299.0850 www.gomamago.com
mon noon - 7p tue - sat 11a - 7 sun noon - 5p

opened in 2001. founder: noi chudnoff owner: jonathan chudnoff
all major credit cards accepted

14th street > s13

For the most part, fusion in food is not for me. When I see chile rellenos and gnocchi on the same menu, my tastebuds get confused. Hmph? Springrolls, sushi and steak au poivre all in one place? Wrong. There is one place, however, where I embrace multicultural fusion wholeheartedly, and that is at *Go Mama Go*, where a gazillion different cultures, designs, styles and attitudes all come together in one place. Use finds from here when you're hosting a party or mixing east and west styles, though take note when it comes to the food—skip mixing the lasagna and laksa.

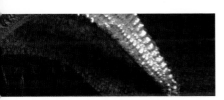

covet:
silver shells
marimekko dish towels
wooden chopsticks
sake sets
original crown mill stationary
tag cheese utensils
bamboo folding fan

good wood

american furniture, decorative arts and really good wood

1428 u street northwest. between 14th and 15th
green: u street / african-american civil war memorial / cardozo
202.986.3640 www.goodwooddc.com
thu 5 - 9p fri - sat 11a - 7p sun 11a - 5p

opened in 1993. owners: anna and daniel kahoe
all major credit cards accepted

u street >

I have had a love affair with all things made of wood since I bought a beat-up farm table to use as a desk my senior year of college. My roommates thought it was an odd choice, but it's been with me ever since, making me love it all the more. As wood ages, it gets well-worn with time and touch, and good wood becomes great wood. This is what *Good Wood* is all about—glorious wooden furniture and decorative arts that have aged exquisitely. When you choose one of Anna and Daniel's hand-picked pieces to bring home, you'll instantaneously feel the added warmth.

covet:
19th century carved walnut dining table
19th century pine seed cabinet
butcher block
pine tool box
two board farm table
early empire chest of drawers
machine part mold

greater goods

green goods for the greater good

1626 u street northwest. between new hampshire and 17th
green : u street / african-american civil war memorial / cardozo
202.449.6070 www.greatergoods.com
tue - sat 11a - 8p sun 11a - 6p

opened in 2007. owner: daniel velez
all major credit cards accepted
classes. contractor resources

How appropriate that I find myself thinking about *Greater Goods* on Earth Day. If April 22 is like Christmas for the earth, then consider *Greater Goods* a year-round Christmas shop for the planet, where you can do good every day just by shopping here. The best part is realizing how much easier and happier these energy-, waste- and water-saving tools and products can make your life. Nothing makes me happier than filling my reusable Sigg bottle and toting my groceries in my Envirosax bag, making green living so much more stylish and good lookin' than the plastic alternative.

covet:
small living by sandra moya
simple human cab mount trash system
mrs. meyers everything
energizer rechargeable batteries
sigg water bottles
envirosax
bag-e-wash plastic bag dryer

green and blue

women's clothing as pretty as a peacock's plume

1350 connecticut avenue northwest. between dupont circle and n
red line: dupont circle
202.223.6644 www.greenandbluestyle.com
mon - fri 10a - 8p sat 11a - 7p sun noon - 6p

opened in 2007. owners: daniela cermanova and michaela schwartz
all major credit cards accepted

dupont circle > **s16**

It's no wonder I was drawn to this store by its name. *Green and Blue* are my favorite colors, and just about the only colors you'll find in my wardrobe other than my usual greyblackbrownkhakicremewhite neutral color wheel. If you're analyzing the color spectrum, you'll find green and blue to be the most soothing. And though the delightful clothing here is in no way limited to these two colors, you will find a peaceful, calming aura and clothes pretty enough to make even a peacock green with envy.

covet:
cynthia steffe silver blouse
shosanna print dress
rebecca taylor silk tank
7 for all mankind gold clutch
citizens of humanity denim
ela ela couture & jewelry
t bags

homebody

shopping for the homebody in you

715 eighth street southeast. between g and i. blue / orange: eastern market
202.544.8445 www.homebodydc.com
tue - sat 11a - 7p sun noon - 6p

opened in 2005. owners: erin mara and henriette fourcade
all major credit cards accepted

capitol hill >  **s17**

I am a homebody, through and through. I love puttering around my house, going from room to room and making things look pretty and put together. Of course, in order to make my place look good to begin with, I need to shop at a place like *Homebody*. This shop fits nearly every need, whether being a homebody to you means luxurious foaming baths or setting an exquisite table. I'll admit that nesting is my preference, but *Homebody* is the ultimate lure to get me to fly the coop.

covet:
self-adhesive panorama of paris
lovegrove & repucci delft dishware
erbaviva organic bath oil
angela adams rugs
tontempi casa furniture
gus modern everything
dani pear vitamin bath soak

home rule

super organized home store

1807 14th street northwest. between s and t
green : u street / african-american civil war memorial / cardozo
202.797.5544 www.homerule.com
mon - sat 11a - 7p sun noon - 5:30p

opened in 1999. owners: greg link and rod glover
all major credit cards accepted
online shopping

14th street > **s18**

I have several rules for my home, especially kitchen-related rules. Only delicious-smelling hand soaps. No unattractive dishcloths. Cooking utensils must be practical *and* beautiful. Only cloth napkins allowed at the table. Cooking must be done with good tools and equipment. There are many more rules, and I could go on and on, but instead let's talk about *Home Rule*, and why I love it so. I can fulfill all of the above needs and the rest of my long list here, which makes my life much more pleasurable than regulatory.

covet:
orange salter scale
chopstick kids
octopus dish scrubber
korres party survival kit
cucina coriander & olive oil hand soap
bamboo cutting boards
blue le creuset dutch oven

hu's shoes

exquisite shoe salon

3005 m street northwest. corner of 30th. orange / blue: foggy bottom / gwu
202.342.0202 www.husshoes.com
mon - sat 11a - 8p sun noon - 5p

opened in 2005. owner: marlene hu aldaba
all major credit cards accepted
online shopping

georgetown > **s19**

My older sister has the most impressive and extensive collection of shoes I have ever known anyone to have. She even has custom-built shoe shelves to house and display them all (well, not quite all; there is never enough room for Sarah's shoes). Her variety of shoes is eclectic, wide-reaching and worthy of an art exhibit. While I can't shop from my sister's closet, I can certainly shop from *Hu's Shoes* which has an even more impressive and covetable collection—and I can actually own the shoes I buy from here. Watch out soon for *Anna's Shoes*.

covet:
maison martin margiela wedge sandals
devi kroell python platform
alejandro ingelmo metallic flats
stella mccartney beaded sandal
lanvin crystal starburst blue flat
elisanero pump with blue heel
barbara bui bags

hysteria

designer, fashion-forward clothing for women

125 south fairfax street. between king and prince. blue / yellow: king street
703.548.1615 www.shophysteria.com
mon - sat 11a - 6p sun noon - 6p and by appointment

opened in 1999. owners: ethan and lindsey drath
all major credit cards accepted
online shopping

alexandria >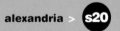

I have two older sisters, and I find that it's nearly impossible not to have bouts of sisterly envy like Cindy did in "The Brady Bunch"—wanting Marcia's hairstyle or Jan's groovy outfit. *Hysteria*—with its exquisitely arranged, pretty dresses and elegant accessories—is like the elder Brady girls. As the youngest, my first reaction might be to feel a bit like the third wheel here, but then I tell myself to quit whining and get buying! I'll take the polished outfits and the sharp shoes, please. Suddenly because of *Hysteria*, I'm a cool Brady girl also, decked out ever-so-stylishly.

covet:
milly chain top
trina turk striped sweater
calypso wrap dress
orla kiely bright stripe dress
tory burch blue straw tote
jack rodgers brown navajo sandal
kenneth jay lane circle link necklace

insight opticians

cool eyeware

1240 f street northwest. between 13th and 12th
blue / orange / red: metro center
202.347.9882 www.insightdc.com
mon - wed 10a - 6p thu 10a - 8p fri 10a - 6p sat noon - 5p

opened in 2005. owners: lynn white and yolanda james
all major credit cards accepted
on-site optometrist

penn quarter > 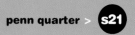 **s21**

When I was at *Insight*, a woman came in to pick up her new glasses. She was so excited to wear the new frames that she came in before work. She was giddy as she admired her new look in the mirrors and left happily with a bounce in her step. I imagine that every eyeglass purchase here has the same results. The frames that fill this shop are so unusual and distinctive, they are bound to give an immediate, stunning makeover. For those of us who don't require glasses, there is an equally delicious sunglass collection. I'm fawning over the Sophia Loren shades now.

covet:
eyeglasses:
  oliver goldsmith
  paul smith
  beausoleil
  loree rodkin
  modern amusement
  cutler and gross
  gotti

la cuisine

a shop for serious cooks and bakers

323 cameron street. between royal and fairfax. blue / yellow: king street
703.836.4435 www.lacuisineus.com
mon - wed 10a - 5p thu 10a - 7p fri 10a - 5p sat 10a - 6p

opened in 1970. owner: nancy purves pollard
all major credit cards accepted
online shopping. classes / events

alexandria >

In *eat.shop paris*, authored by Monsieur Jon Hart, there is a cooking shop called *E. Dehillerin*. I've stared long and hard at Jon's photographs of shiny copper pots, stacks of doilies, and longed for what he notes as "the best wooden spoons in the world." Back from a recent Paris trip, my sisters brought me one of these coveted wooden spoons, which I treasure while waiting until I can make a pilgrimage there. Then I found *La Cuisine*. Wait. They have the same best wooden spoons in the world! And shiny copper pots! You'll be hard-pressed to find a better cook's shop this side of the Atlantic.

covet:
the best:
  copper molds
  cookie cutters
  wooden spoons
whisks galore
india tree murray river salt
maple, cherry & alder smoking chips
les confitures à l'ancienne chocolat en poudre

meeps vintage fashionette

fabulous vintage for women and men

2104 18th street northwest. between callifornia and wyoming

red: dupont circle

202.265.6546 www.meepsdc.com

mon - sat noon - 7p sun noon - 5p

opened in 1992. owners: danni sharkey and leann trowbridge

all major credit cards accepted

adams morgan > **s23**

When I was little, I used to get hand-me-downs from my two older sisters. At that point in my life, this was not a desirable arrangement. I wanted new clothes! My own clothes! Now, I see hand-me-downs from my stylish sisters as one of the greatest resources for my wardrobe. If you don't have your own siblings who let you clean out their closets from time to time, think of *Meeps* as a big brother or sister, one with vintage shoes, clothes and accessories that will add something special to your collection. And in this closet, everything's fair game—whatever you choose, is all yours.

covet:
white buckle shoes
great retro sunglass selection
ruffle headpiece
tweed coats
bright blue pumps
faux fur hats
vintage kids' clothing
local designers' clothing

miss pixie's furnishings & whatnot

good old stuff and whatnots

1626 14th street northwest. corner of r
green: u street / african-american civil war memorial / cardozo
202.232.8171 www.misspixies.com
thu - sun noon - 7p

opened in 1997. owner: pixie windsor
all major credit cards accepted

adams morgan > **s24**

I love the shiny, the new, the just-released. But sometimes I imagine a world that is a material eco-system of sorts, where nothing is wasted or thrown out. People would buy, borrow, trade and swap their goods. When you needed a new couch, you would shop from friends, family, neighbors, or coworkers, and the whole world could be your store. Though we're working on it, this country is still quite a way from such a concept. In the meantime, *Miss Pixie's*— filled with used and well-loved stuff, now yours for a deal—comes closest. Waste not, want not.

covet:
school chairs
vintage b & w photos
garden ornament
wooden folding chairs
chinese tins
regensburg ashtray
blue velvet chair

muléh

a moden lifestyle store for the sartorial set

1831 14th street northwest. between s and t
green: u street / african-american civil war memorial / cardozo
202.667.3440 www.muleh.com
tue - sat 11a - 7p sun noon - 5p

opened in 2004. owners: christopher l. reiter and vici subiyant
all major credit cards accepted

14th street > **s25**

I spend most of the summer outside of the city. Life is simplified and days are spent mostly outdoors. When I return home at the end of the summer, I want to bring part of this lake life home with me. At *Muléh*, they have the items that would help me achieve this goal: clean-lined furniture crafted of natural woods and materials and non-fussy, yet beautiful clothing. Creating a lifestyle via this store, with its naturally graceful style, would be just the cure for my longing for summer to return. Now if only I could do something about the nasty winter weather...

covet:
neo prim console
chiquita stools
chrysalis sky floor lamp
rozae nichols purple goddess dress
lauren moffat crochet top
common thread dresses
philip lim 3.1 dresses

nana

new and vintage styles for women

1528 u street northwest. between 15th and 16th
green: u street / african-american civil war memorial / cardozo
202.667.6955 www.nanadc.com
mon - sat noon - 7p sun noon - 5p

opened in 2003. owner: jackie flanagan
all major credit cards accepted
online shopping

u street > s26

These days, clothing prices seem to be rising as quickly as gas prices, skyrocketing out of control (sometimes it seems like $100 per inch), leaving you wondering how to stay up on trends without spending an entire paycheck. The answer is *Nana*! This sweet store is filled with adorable niceties, made even nicer by the fact that not every price tag engenders near coronary arrest due to sticker shock. Now the only problem is that you may want everything here, making you spend the bulk of that paycheck after all. Ah well, nothing better than supporting a local business like *Nana*.

covet:
porridge green dress
dagg & stacey coats
hobo belts
la made black ruched jacket
la made t's
holly aiken bags
san diego hat co. hats

palace 5ive

killer kicks (and boards) for killer tricks
2216-2220 14th street northwest. between florida and w
green: u street / african-american civil war memorial / cardozo
202.299.9008 www.palace5ive.com
mon - sat 11a - 9p sun noon - 6p

opened in 2008. owner: greg grammen
all major credit cards accepted

u street >

To be candid with you, I've never been on a board of any kind—skate, surf or snow. But this doesn't mean that I can't appreciate the downright coolness of this store. To the skaters out there, *Palace 5ive* is a place to buy imperative supplies. To me and fellow non-skaters, this store is a fantastic gallery to be admired. For example, I find myself seriously coveting the skate sneaks. I feel like I don't have to be a skater to wear these shoes. It's not as though everyone who's ever worn running shoes runs, right? Right. Skater or not, come and see one of the coolest spots in town.

covet:
vans "off the wall" green sneaks
checkerboard vans
creative recreation white hi-tops
silver velcro creative recreation shoes
small, medium large
dc red shoes
stussy black & white skateboard

147

political americana

politcal paraphernalia for both parties

1331 pennsylvania avenue northwest. corner of 14th
blue / orange / red: metro center
202.737.7730 www.politicalamericana.com
mon - sat 9a - 8p sun 10a - 6p

opened about 25 years ago. owner: jim warlick
all major credit cards accepted
online shopping

penn quarter > **s28**

DC is the capital of the United States, isn't it? And the release of this book corresponds to a presidential election year, doesn't it? Answers are yes and yes, which means this store is the spot to pick up bumper stickers, presidential playing cards and campaign buttons. *Political Americana* isn't just for election-year voters, but also for the true collectors, for whom politics and presidents are like a sporting event and its players. Whether for a pair of cufflinks worn by JFK or for a simple partisan postcard, all voters will enjoy *Political Americana*, elephants and donkeys alike.

covet:
elephant & donkey golf balls
dukakis bubblegum cigars
hillary & obama playing cards
military cufflinks
vintage political buttons
fdr campaign banner
white house christmas ornament
fbi divot set

pop

pop fashion for women and men

1803a 14th street northwest. corner of s
green: u street / african american - civil war memorial / cardozo
202.332.3312 www.shoppop.com
mon - sat 11a - 7p sun noon - 6p

opened in 2003. owner: sheila sharma
all major credit cards accepted

14th street >

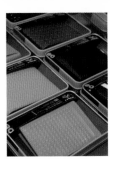

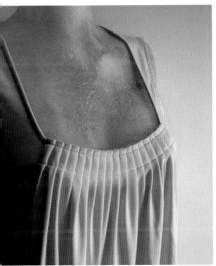

I love Madonna. And Justin Timberlake. And I'm obsessed with the Olsen twins. And I like to sneak a peak at the weekly glossies while in line at the grocery store. Yes, I'm a sucker for all things pop—pop culture, pop music, pop magazines, pop fashion. It's all so sweetly addictive, I can't seem to quit. *Pop*, the store, is one you won't want to quit either as it's filled with pop-culture couture, minus eye-popping prices. Plus, Sheila orders very few multiples, which means way less of a chance you'll end up in an *Us Weekly*-esque column titled "Who Wore It Better?" Phew.

covet:
white latico bag
goorin hats
white-rimmed sunglasses
j. fold orange wallet
paul frank striped gloves
cloth-covered bangles
free people tights
chinese laundry black-patent shoes

151

rckndy

sweet design for the home

1515 u street northwest. between 15th and 16th
green: u street / african-american civil war memorial / cardozo
202.332.5639 www.rckndy.com
tue - thu 11a - 7p fri - sat 10a - 8p sun noon - 6p

opened in 2007. owner: david dennis
all major credit cards accepted

u street >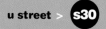

Rckndy and rock candy have a few things in common: they are both brightly colorful, sweetly appealing, and completely crave-able. Now here are the major differences between *Rckndy* and rock candy: while one rots your teeth, spoils your appetite and adds empty calories, the other enhances your living space, beautifies your life, and adds goodness along with sweetness. In other words, *Rckndy* is good for you! Good design is good for all! And the best news of all: you don't ever need to go on some crazy diet from the delicious treats you'll find here.

covet:
mud australia ceramics
orange 22 white table
egg planters
alessi salt & pepper shakers
kol bath sea salts
time flies clocks
blu dot red desk set

redeem

fresh, bold and unique casual wear for both sexes

1734 14th street northwest. between s and r
green: u street / african-american civil war memorial / cardozo
202.332.7447 www.redeemus.com
mon noon - 8p wed - sat noon - 8p sun noon - 6p

opened in 2006. owner: lori parkerson
all major credit cards accepted

14th street >  **s31**

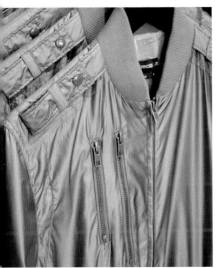

I like it when a store takes on responsibilities—beyond offering stylish goods—and becomes an integral piece of the fabric of a city. *Redeem* starts with a motivating tag line: it's never too late to change. The aim is to assist in the neighborhood's revitalization while at the same time while outfitting the whole city in cool, urban duds. *Redeem* is more than a shop; it's a way of life that involves hosting knit nites, supporting indie designers, and offering a forum for local artists and charities. Whether it's your soul or your style that needs a changing, *Redeem* is the place for you.

covet:
orthodox gunmetal jacket
religion grey & blue striped shirt
colcci purple ankle boots
de nana pompom knit scarf
corpus black hooded sweater
corpus japanese rope scarf
ernest sewn denim

relish

a well-dressed shop for the well heeled

3312 cadys alley northwest. at 33rd and m
orange / blue : foggy bottom / gwu
202.333.5343 www.relishdc.com
mon - wed 10a - 6p thu 10a - 7p fri - sat 10a - 6p

opened in 1996. owner: nancy pearlstein
all major credit cards accepted

georgetown >  **s32**

No trip to DC feels quite right without doing these three things: riding the metro and admiring Harry Weese's impressive stations; strolling the National Mall and admiring the Washington Monument; and going to Georgetown to admire *Relish*. Tucked away in Cady's Alley off of busy M street, this shop is unlike any other local shop you may find, in beauty, in beauty or breadth of covetable designer wear. To me, it's as much a sight to see as any national monument. If those memorials mark victories of past history, think of *Relish* for fashion victories of the present and future.

covet:
nili lotan white sundress
nicole fahri buttery leather bags
robert clergerie purple suede wedges
marni painted horn chili bracelet
martin margiela red leather bag
dries van noten belts
jill platner jewelry
james perse t's

sangaree

independent women's clothing

3288 m street northwest. between 33rd and potomac
blue / orange: foggy bottom-gwu
202.333.4690 www.sangareeboutique.com
mon - sat 10a - 7p sun 11a - 6p

opened in 2007. owner: churek dzhamgerchinova
all major credit cards accepted

georgetown >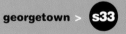

When you ask folks where to shop in DC, they inevitably point you in the direction of Georgetown. How could they not? Every major retailer you could want is within Wisconsin and M. Don't get me wrong—I love the big guys (they were small guys at one point, after all), but I am very sad to see the little independents being pushed out. Not *Sangaree* though! Here is a success story of a small shop going for it, and on the main drag to boot. So when big becomes boring to you in Georgetown, march yourself here, where you'll find amazing clothing and small-biz charm.

covet:
alvin valley:
   jacket & skirt suit
   navy tie-neck dress
   wide leg blue pants
derecuny pleated pink dress
navy matt & nat handbag
ports tweed jacket
sade streamline hot pink large clutch

tabletop

functional objects for all surfaces

1608 20th street northwest. corner of q
red: dupont circle
202.387.7117 www.tabletopdc.com
mon - sat noon - 8p sun noon - 6p

opened in 2003. owners: tai tsang, daphne olive, and dubi paltshik
all major credit cards accepted
online shopping. gift registry

dupont circle > **s34**

I have favorite places to visit in DC for satisfying the art-history student in me: the National Gallery of Art, the Corcoran Gallery of Art and *Tabletop*. Okay, so you won't find any Andy Warhol or Winslow Homer here, and no, *Tabletop* isn't a museum, but it's a great place to purchase items for your home from the thriving world of art and design. Who knows? Many items here may grace the design wings of museums in the future. If you go nowhere else in DC for a cultural outing, come here. *Tabletop's* got one of the best design collections around.

covet:
snow & graham candles
deco breeze bright orange fan
pare umbrellas
marimekko everything
lotta jansdotter aprons
kit + lili canvas owl bag
heavenly body pisces perfume

teaism

a tea shop

400 eighth street northwest. corner of d
green / yellow: archives-navy memorial
202.638.6010 www.teaism.com
mon - fri 10a - 6p sat - sun 11a - 6p
(see eat side for teaism tea house information)

opened in 1996. owners: michelle brown and linda neumann
all major credit cards accepted
online shopping.

penn quarter > **s35**

It is a true pleasure to hang out at the home of *eat.
shop* head honcho Kaie Wellman. One of the main
reasons is that in her kitchen is a drawer of tea that
has such a multitude of varieties, leaves, and coun-
tries represented, she could probably open her own
tea shop. Thanks to *Teaism,* you don't have to break
into Kaie's house and go scrounging in her stash—
you can create your own magnificent tea collection
purchasing from here, where the selection of loose-
leaf teas in ornate boxes is bound to keep your tea
cravings happy.

covet:
teas:
  ceylon
  organic earl grey
  pu'er tuo cha
  golden dragon
  bi luo chun
stump teapot
japanese tea scoop

163

terra

a gift box of a boutique

1706 connecticut avenue northwest. between r and s. red: dupont circle
202.232.8581 www.shopterradc.com
mon - sat 11a - 8p sun noon - 5p

opened in 2006. owner: oriana khatso
mc. visa
online shopping (via email or phone). style tune up. in-store styling

dupont circle > s36

When I entered *Terra*, I immediately became so enamored with a Rebecca Minkoff satchel (part utility, part pure and straightforward elegance) that even though I wandered through the store, I kept aiming back to it, aching to own it. On my second full lap around the store, I spied the colorful lacquer bangles and was then torn between bangles and bag. This is indicative of *Terra*—a place so full of good finds, that suddenly you're coveting beyond reason. This is the perfect sort of place to spoil yourself and others mightily.

covet:
j brand jeans
oscar de la renta island candle
lia kes button down
elizabeth w luxuries set
rebecca minkoff satchel
terry stack belts
panda snack bamboo t's

the brass knob

brass knobs and architectural antiques and salvage

2311 18th street northwest. between kalorama and columbia
red : dupont circle / woodley park-zoo / adams morgan
202.332.3370 www.thebrassknob.com
mon - sat 10:30a - 6p sun noon - 5p

opened in 1991. owner: donetta george
all major credit cards accepted
online shopping

adams morgan > **s37**

I grew up in a Tudor home built in the '30s, with more than 50 brass doorknobs throughout. My parents deemed it an exciting Saturday outing to go hunting for the prettiest and most stately brass knobs to fit our home. So when I first set foot into *The Brass Knob*, my jaw dropped in awe of the hundreds of shiny, intricate and stunning knobs. I hope someday my parents get a chance to visit here, but secretly I'm thankful they live on the opposite coast as my Saturdays would be spoken for once again, shopping with them to find more brass beauties from *The Brass Knob*.

covet:
every sort of brass doorknob imaginable
fireplace mantels
cast-iron brackets
concrete pineapple finials
classical revival chandelier
stained glass
minton tiles

the magic wardrobe

exceptional clothing for kids

1663 wisconsin avenue northwest. between q and r
blue / orange: foggy bottom / gwu
202.333.0353 www.themagicwardrobe.com
mon - sat 10a - 5p sun noon - 5p

opened in 1989. owner: bridget c. wilson
all major credit cards accepted
online shopping

georgetown >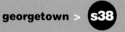

Do you remember your favorite outfit when you were little? Or maybe a beloved pair of shoes? I remember a pair of pale pink sandals I had and wore with everything I could until I sadly outgrew them. I think every little girl and boy should have at least one favorite childhood shirt, sweater, or pretty little dress that lodges in his or her memory. *The Magic Wardrobe* is the place to find those special pieces. Bridget handpicks everything here, piece by carefully crafted piece, creating a collection of children's clothing that is far away from ordinary.

covet:
bella bliss seersucker dress
cantebury of new zealand rugby shirts
little marc everything
hartford oxford
little piggy silver flats
bonpoint cashmere sweaters
pap d'anjo seersucker jumpers

the old print gallery

antique prints and maps

1220 31st street northwest. between n and m
blue / orange: foggy bottom / gwu
202.965.1818 www.oldprintgallery.com
mon - sat 10a - 5:30p

opened in 1971. owner: judy blakely
all major credit cards accepted
online shopping (by phone or fax). paper conservation / restoration services
appraisals. framing

georgetown > **s39**

Ever since my husband gave me a centuries-old map of the world for our anniversary, I have become infatuated with maps. So when *The Old Print Gallery* came across my radar, I knew immediately that it would be hard to tear myself away. The store is filled with shelves of vintage maps and prints, organized by category. It's captivating to gaze at old maps to see what a place looked like ages ago, to find the familiar spots that suprisingly haven't changed for centuries. If you're like me, you'll need to give yourself hours here to get lost traveling back through time.

covet:
prints:
  american portraits
  new england city views
  architecture
  gardens
maps:
  united states
  foreign

the remix

remixed vintage styles
645 pennsylvania avenue southeast. between 6th and 7th
blue / orange: eastern market
202.547.0211 www.remixvintage.com
mon - fri 11a - 7p sat 11a - 8p sun noon - 6p

opened in 2002. owner: stacey a. ditata
all major credit cards accepted
online shopping

capitol hill >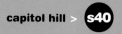

As I was shooting *The Remix*, a friendly and downright euphoric Irish woman and mother-of-the-groom-to-be began telling me the story of her search for a dress for her son's wedding. She'd searched in multiple cities and finally had found the most lovely pale green (she's Irish, after all) gown at *The Remix*. This reminded me why I love vintage shops so much—the possibility that a true gem might be discovered, one that will be unique to you yet shares a connection to someone before you. That's a true love story if you ask me.

covet:
'60s molly parnis beaded gown
'50s big eye levi's jacket
pink feather hat
gold-rimmed sunglassees
elvis lamp
black & white ruffled shirt
sequined, strapless pink dress

the shoe hive

a shoe shop that's the bee's knees

115 south royal street. between king and prince
blue / yellow: king street
703.548.7105 www.theshoehive.com
mon - sat 11a - 6p sun noon - 5p

opened in 2003. owner: elizabeth todd
all major credit cards accepted
online shopping

alexandria >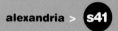

Shoes aren't unlike bees in a hive. In a hive, there are the worker bees, the drones and the queen bee. I generally organize shoes into similar categories. The drone of shoes is one that has little real function, that is all about sitting around and being pretty. The worker bee of shoes is the one that you can walk for miles in, that you pack for a trip. And the queen bee of shoes is the one you wake up thinking about wearing. *The Shoe Hive* has a shoe for whatever your need. The only dilemma is what happens when there is more than one queen bee in a hive?

covet:
lulu guiness gunmetal silver pumps
hollywould gold lizard embossed peep toe
tory burch green flip-flops
michael kors brown leather flats
matiko navy patent flats
loeffler randall navy peep toes
dkny ballet flats

tone on tone

painted antiques and accessories

7920 woodmont avenue. between fairmont and saint elmo. red line: bethesda
240.497.0800 www.tone-on-tone.com
mon - sat 11a - 5p

opened in 2005. owners: thomas troeschel and loi thai
all major credit cards accepted

bethesda >

There was a summer in college I spent painting every piece of furniture I could get my hands on white. I have always had a penchant for all tonalities of white, so you can imagine how my jaw-dropped when I set foot into *Tone on Tone*. While I am nothing but an over-zealous amateur with a paintbrush, this place is filled with true masterpieces of 18th and 19th century painted antiques, with nary a color in sight. Hopefully you have a place in your home for one of these patina-ed beauties—but if you don't, just come to admire the pristine splendor.

covet:
danish classical settee
gustavian painted bench
early swedish cabinet
french zinc table
painted blanket chest
white rococo table
french gothic mirror
french painted ladder

tschiffely pharmacy

old-world pharmacy carrying traditional and non-traditional remedies
dc: 1330 connecticut avenue northwest. between n and dupont circle. 202.331.7176
us: 50 massachussetts avenue northeast. in union station. 202.408.5178
dc > red: dupont circle / us > red: union station
www.rxdc.com
please see website for hours and third location

opened in 1874. owners: david toth, paul d. gambino, robert m. nelson and john j. burns
all major credit cards accepted

dupont circle / union station > s43

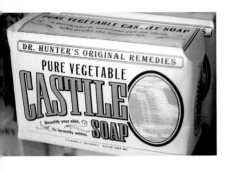

While my dad is a doctor of Western medicine, my mom has always flirted with the role of Eastern practitioner. For headaches and stuffed sinuses, she'd rub Tiger Balm on our temples and under our noses. For stomachaches, she'd give us pieces of ginger to chew. When I got super sick, my dad called in a prescription, and my mom made herbal tea. My parents covered all the bases, and *Tschiffely Pharmacy* does, too. You can get traditional pharmacy needs filled here, but you'll also find alternative cures and medicinal balms. This is where East and West meet in a perfect balance of yin and yang.

covet:
dr. unters original pure vegetable castille soap
pinaud lilac vegetal aftershave lotion
tiger balm
sloan's liniment
essential oils
grether's blackcurrant pastilles
caswell-massey's elixir of love
ahava mandarin-cedarwood bath salts

tugooh toys

stylish natural toys

1419 wisconsin avenue. between o and p
blue / orange: foggy bottom / gwu
202.333.0032 www.yirostores.com
mon - sat 10a - 6p sun 11a - 5p

opened in 2007
all major credit cards accepted

georgetown > **s44**

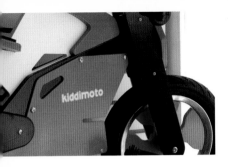
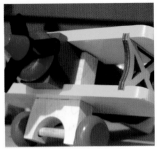

My husband and I are in an idealistic, pre-parenting state, where we imagine our future babies clad in pristine duds, playing only with exquisitely designed wooden toys—and if by chance a plastic enticement comes their way they will clearly state, "No, thanks. I prefer the cool wooden toys." Okay, it's a fantasy, but *Tugooh Toys* makes it not that far-fetched. They carry eco smart, well-designed toys that tykes really (!!) want to play with. Believe me, there's not a kid alive who wouldn't want to zoom around on that super cool red kiddimoto bike I was eyeing.

covet:
art supplies galore
playmobil
haba bead abacus
sitch scooter
vilac cars
model airplanes
alex needlecraft kit
automoblox mini cars

yiro

an organic baby shop

3236 p street northwest. between o and p. blue / orange: foggy bottom / gwu
202.338.9476 www.yirostores.com
mon - sat 10a - 6p sun 11a - 5p

opened in 2007
all major credit cards accepted
concierge services

georgetown > **s45**

If you happen to keep up with the news du jour, every other story seems to be about products that are hazardous to our health and, of even more concern, our kids' health. It can certainly be overwhelming—not to mention joy-draining—to shop under such strict protocols for what you should and shouldn't be using or wearing, especially when you're shopping for two. *Yiro*, which is the sibling store to *Tugooh Toys*, knows exactly what is good for you and your baby, so you can relax and actually enjoy shopping once again. Phew.

covet:
maclaren beginning alleviating leg lotion
mama mio deluxe pampering
under the nile striped organic onesies
purebaby receiving blankets
the laundress baby detergent
zmooz organic cotton doll
trebimbi puppets utensils
adiri natural baby bottle

notes

etc.

the eat.shop guides were created by kaie wellman and are published by cabazon books

for more information about the series, or to buy print or online books, please visit: eatshopguides.com

eat.shop washington dc 2nd edition was written, researched and photographed by anna h. blessing

editing: kaie wellman   copy editing: lynn king   fact checking: emily mattson
map and layout production: julia dickey

anna thx: the businesses in this book, for being so welcoming. kaie, for creating these books to begin with.

cabazon books: eat.shop washington dc 2nd edition
ISBN-13 978-0-9799557-4-7

copyright 2008 © cabazon books

all rights reserved under international and pan-american copyright conventions. no part of this
publication may be reproduced, stored in a retrieval system, or transmitted in any form or by any
means, electronic, mechanical, photocopying, recording or otherwise, without prior written
permission of the copyright owner.

every effort has been made to ensure the accuracy of the information in this book. however, certain details
are subject to change. please remember when using the guides that hours alter seasonally and sometimes
sadly, businesses close. the publisher cannot accept responsibility for any consequences arising from the
use of this book.

the eat.shop guides are distributed by independent publishers group: www.ipgbook.com

PRINTED IN CHINA